TRY NOT TO LAUGHT!

68 Jokes

What happens when leprechauns take a bath?

They get wet!

What do you get when you do the Irish jig at McDonalds?

A Shamrock Shake!

HOW DO LEPRECHAUNS CELEBRATE ST. PATRICK'S DAY?

BY HOLDING A LEPRECONCERT!

JOKE BOOK

KNOCK, KNOCK!

WHO'S THERE?

PAT.

PAT WHO?

PAT ON YOUR SHOES AND LET'S GET TO THE ST. PATRICK'S DAY PARTY!

How do leprechauns celebrate
St. Patrick's Day?

By holding a lepreconcert!

JOKE BOOK

Knock, knock!

Who's there?

Pat.

Pat who?

Pat on your shoes and let's get
to the St. Patrick's Day party!

Why did the leprechaun open his umbrella?

He walked under a rainbow!

JOKE BOOK

Where did the lazy leprechaun find gold?

In the dictionary!

What would you get if
you crossed a leprechaun
with a frog?

A little man having a
hopping good time!

JOKE BOOK

How did the leprechaun
beat the Irishman to the
pot of gold?

He took a short cut!

Why are so many
leprechauns gardeners?

they have green
thumbs!

JOKE BOOK

How did the Irish Jig get
started?

Too much water to drink
and not enough
restrooms!

knock knock

Who's there?

Irish! Irish Who?

Irish you a happy St. Patrick's Day.

JOKE BOOK

Why can't you borrow money from a leprechaun?

Because they're always a little short!

What did St. Patrick say to the snakes?

He told them to hiss off.

JOKE BOOK

What would you get if you crossed Christmas with St. Patrick's Day?

St. O'Claus!

What's Irish and
stays out all night?

Paddy O'Furniture

JOKE BOOK

How do you know if an
Irishman is having fun?

He's Dublin over with
laughter!

What is Dwayne
Johnson's Irish
nickname?

The Sham-Rock.

JOKE BOOK

What did the naughty
leprechaun get for
Christmas?

A pot of coal!

Why are leprechauns so hard to get along with?

Because they are short tempered!

JOKE BOOK

Why did the leprechaun stand on the potato?

To keep from falling in the stew!

Why should you never iron a four-leaf clover?

You don't want to press your luck

JOKE BOOK

Who was St. Patrick's favorite superhero?

Green Lantern.

What do you call a
diseased criminal?

A leper-con!

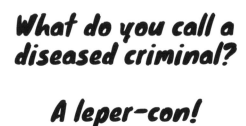

JOKE BOOK

When is an Irish potato
not an Irish potato?

When it's a French fry!

How did the Irish Jig get started?

Too much water to drink and not enough restrooms!

JOKE BOOK

Why do leprechauns make great secretaries?

They're good at shorthand.

Why did St. Patrick drive the snakes out of Ireland?

Because he couldn't afford a plane ticket.

JOKE BOOK

Do people get jealous of the Irish?

Yes, they're green with envy!

What kind of music do
leprechauns love?

Sham-rock

JOKE BOOK

What's an Irishman's
favorite room in the
house?

The Paddy O'!

Why do leprechauns dislike leftovers?

They prefer left-clovers!

JOKE BOOK

What do you call an Irish spider?

Paddy O' Long Legs

What does it mean when you find a horseshoe?

A poor horse is going barefoot!

JOKE BOOK

Why did St. Patrick drive all the snakes out of Ireland?

He couldn't afford their air fare!

What do you call a big
Irish spider?

Paddy long legs!

JOKE BOOK

What happens when a
leprechaun falls into a
river?

He gets wet, of course.

Why did St. Patrick
drive all the snakes
out of Ireland?

He couldn't afford
plane fare!

JOKE BOOK

What is Irish and left
out on the lawn all
summer?

Paddy O'Furniture!

What does a leprechaun call a man wearing green?

A Green Giant.

JOKE BOOK

What type of spells do Irish witches cast?

Lucky charms.

What is a huge Irish
spider called?

Paddy Long Legs

JOKE BOOK

Why do Irish people
recycle?

They like to go green!

knock-knock!

Who's there?
Warren.

Warren who?

Warren anything green
for St. Patrick's Day?

JOKE BOOK

What would you get if
you crossed a
leprechaun with a
Texan?

A pot of chili at the end
of the rainbow!

What's big and purple and lies next to Ireland?

Grape Britain!

JOKE BOOK

Why do people wear shamrocks on St. Patrick's Day?

Regular rocks are too heavy

What happens when a leprechaun falls into a river?

He gets wet!

JOKE BOOK

Why do frogs and alligators like St. Patrick's Day?

Because they are already wearing green!

Why do people wear shamrocks on St. Patrick's Day?

Regular rocks are too heavy

JOKE BOOK

Why do leprechauns hate running?

They'd rather jig than jog!

How can you tell if a
leprechaun is having a
good time?

He is Dublin over with
laughter!

JOKE BOOK

What did the
leprechaun do for a
living?

He was a short-order
cook!

What does it mean if you find a four-leaf clover?

That you have too much time on your hands!

JOKE BOOK

What do leprechauns barbecue on St. Patrick's Day?

Short ribs

Why are leprechauns so concerned about global warming?

They're really into green living

JOKE BOOK

What instrument does a showoff play on St. Patrick's Day?

Bragpipes!

What is a leprechaun's favorite type of music?

Sham-rock 'n' roll!

JOKE BOOK

"Mom, I met an Irishman on St. Patrick's Day."

"Oh, really?"

"No, O'Reilly!"

Why do frogs love St. Patrick's Day?

They're always wearing green

JOKE BOOK

What do you call a bad Irish dance?

A jig mistake

What do you call
environmentally
conscious leprechauns?

Wee-cyclers

JOKE BOOK

How should you buy
drinks on St. Patrick's
Day?

With soda bread

What did the leprechaun say when the video game ended?

Game clover!

JOKE BOOK

What do ghosts drink on St. Patrick's Day?

BOOs!

How did the leprechaun
win the race?

He took a shortcut.

JOKE BOOK

Do leprechauns make
good secretaries?

Sure, they're great at
shorthand!

One last thing...

We would love to hear your feedback about this book!

If you enjoyed this book or found it useful, we would be very grateful if you posted a short review on Amazon. Your support does make a difference and we read every review personally.

If you would like to leave a review, all you need to do is click the review link on this book's page on Amazon

Thank you for your support!

www.enjoydiscovering.net.pl